M000189963

PHOBOPHOB!A

by hat-trick design

KNOCK
KNOCK®
VENICE, CALIFORNIA

Created and designed by hat-trick design
Published by Knock Knock
Distributed by Who's There Inc.
Venice, CA 90291
knockknockstuff.com
Knock Knock is a trademark of Who's There Inc.

Illustrated by hat-trick design
www.hat-trickdesign.co.uk
@hattrick_design

This book is a leisure-time activity book meant solely
for entertainment purposes. In no event will Knock
Knock be liable to any reader for any bodily harm,
injury, or damages, including direct, indirect, incidental,
special, consequential, or punitive arising out of or in
connection with the use of the activities contained in
this book. So there.

Every reasonable attempt has been made to identify
owners of copyright. Errors or omissions will be
corrected in subsequent editions.

Where specific company, product, and brand names
are cited, copyright and trademarks associated with
these names are property of their respective owners.

ISBN: 978-160106485-1
UPC: 825703-50013-4

10 9 8 7 6 5 4 3 2 1

For Becky (buttons and snakes)
Lucille (polystyrene and eyes)
Jessica (spiders and statues)

As someone who is scared of spiders (and snakes and cows and dancing) I wanted to produce a book confronting my fears and those of others.

The word "phobia" comes from the Greek phóbos, meaning "fear" or "morbid fear." In evolutionary terms, fear is a rational instinct. It's the ability to sense danger and confront or run away from it. I generally prefer running away.

But fear can also produce an irrational response: the nightmarish one of freezing to the spot and being unable to respond to the danger.

Its causes can be equally irrational. In clinical terms, a phobia is a serious anxiety disorder that escalates out of proportion to the level of danger, if any exists.

On a more everyday level, phobias are milder, but span a similar range from semirational to outlandish. We all have them. Yours may be in the pages to follow.

Jim Sutherland*
hat-trick design

*Scriptophobia: fear of writing in public

Fear has many eyes and can see things underground.
　　　　　　　　—Miguel de Cervantes

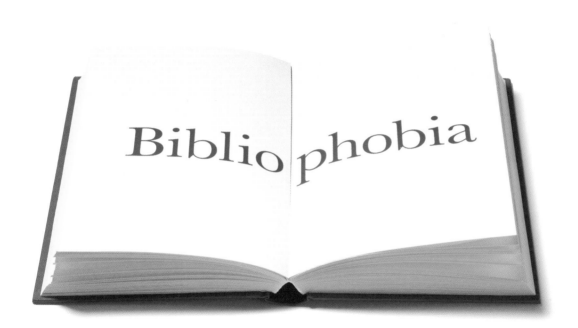

fear of books

Arachnophobia

fear of spiders

PTER ONAR COPH OBIA

fear of flies

fear of peanut butter sticking to the roof of your mouth

fear of meat

LACTO PHOBIA

fear of milk

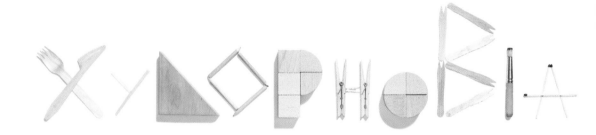

fear of wooden objects

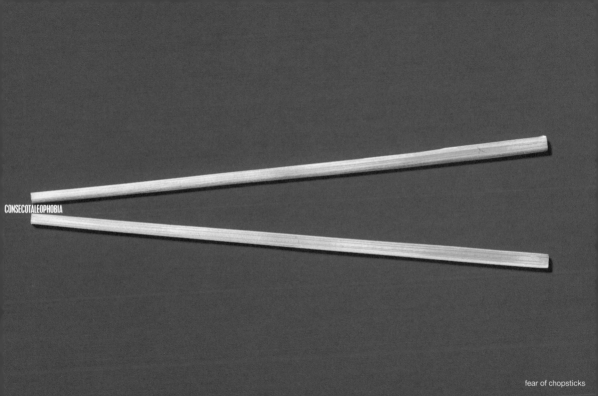

CONSECOTALEOPHOBIA

fear of chopsticks

APHEPH●BIA

fear of being touched

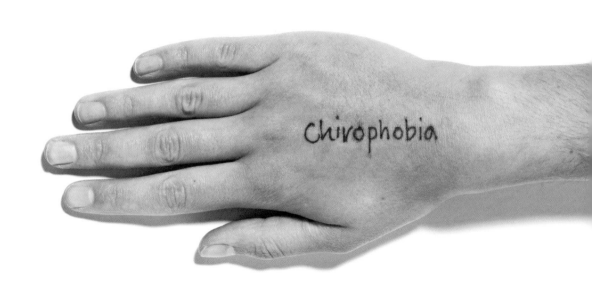

chirophobia

fear of hands

HELIOPHOBIA

fear of the sun

NO（ TIPHOBIA

fear of the night

A⚡traphobia

fear of lightning

Ombrophobia

fear of rain

Ailurophobia

fear of cats

fear of dogs

AVIOPHOBIA ✈ →

fear of flying

WICC🎩PHOBIA

fear of witches

AGYRO

PHOBIA

... crossing the road

AMAXOPHOBIA

fear of riding in a car

Cycloph bia

fear of cycling

Cath󰀀sophobia

fear of sitting

Ambulophobia

fear of walking

ACROPHOBIA

fear of heights

fear of depths

BATHOPHOBIA

CLIMA CO PHOBIA

fear of stairs

H₂YDROPHOBIA

fear of water

METHY PHOBIA

fear of alcohol

OMMETA
PHOBIA

fear of eyes

SCOPO
PHOBIA

fear of being looked at

DIDASKA LEINO- PHOBIA

ERG⬦PHOBIⓐ

fear of work

Logophobia ▶ (noun)
['lȯg-ə-'fō-bē-ə]
plural logophobias
fear of words

TRISKAIDEKA
PHOBIA

fear of the number thirteen

Hippopotomons

osesquipedaliophob

AMATHO PHOBIA

fear of dust

Pteronophobia

fear of being tickled by feathers

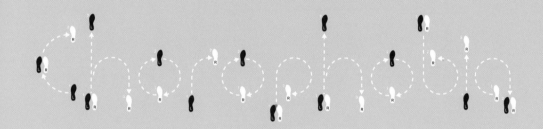

fear of dancing

fear of balloons

fear of loud noises

OPHIDIOPHOBIA OPHIDIOPHOBIA OPHIDIOPHOBIA OPHIDIOPHOBIA OPHIDIOPHOBIA

fear of snakes

STEPNOPHOBIA

fear of ladders

XYROPHOBIA

fear of razors

POGONO PHOBIA

fear of beards

**rnithophobia**

fear of birds

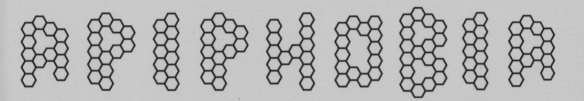

APIPHOBIA

fear of bees

Nudophobia

fear of nudity

Vesti hobia

fear of clothes

Koumpu

nophobia

fear of buttons

BROMIDRO
PHOBIA

fear of body odor

ABLUTOPHOBIA

fear of washing

Chaeto phobia

fear of hair

Catoptro
phobia

fear of mirrors

GNOMOPHOBI

fear of gnomes

Pterido$\wp$o$\wp$hobia

fear of ferns

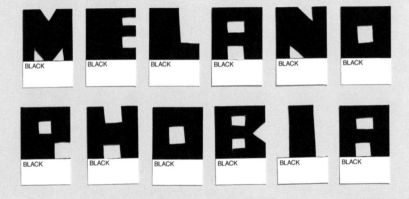

fear of black

GOLD

 LILAC

 LIME

 RED

 MAGENTA

 YELLOW

 NAVY

 GREEN

 CYAN

 PURPLE

 SAFFRON

 BLUE

 ORANGE

 MAROON

fear of color

DENTOPHOBIA

fear of dentists

LAL🗨PH◯BIA

fear of · speaking

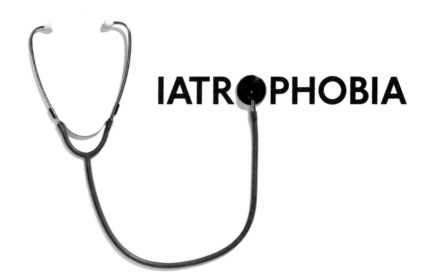

IATROPHOBIA

fear of doctors

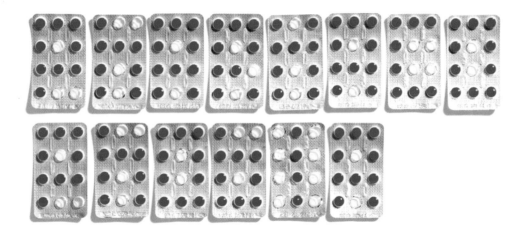

fear of medicine

⊢RYPANOPHOBI⟩——

fear of injections

HEMA-TO-PHOB+IA

fear of blood

SYMMETR

fear of symmetry

Musophobia

fear of mice

TUROPHOBIA

fear of cheese

Taurophobia

fear of bulls

ERYTHROPHOBIA

fear of red

fear of computers

ΗΞιιΞηθιθϱθφλθβΪΔ

fear of Greek or scientific terminology

COULROPHOBIA

fear of clowns

GELIOP**H**OBI**A**!

fear of laughter

fear of paper

AICHMOPHOBIA

fear of sharp objects

fear of time

Tachcophob

fear of speed

fear of men
fear of women

GAM🔗PH🔗BIA

fear of marriage

linena

phobia

fear of string

CHIROPTOPHOBIA

fear of bats

spectrophobia

fear of ghosts

SCIOPHOBIA

fear of shadows

THANATOPHOBIA

R.I.P.

fear of death

PHOBOPHOBIA

AAAAAAH!

Do the thing you fear most
and the death of fear is certain.
— Mark Twain

Image credits in order of appearance

Arachnophobia
Spider, iStockphoto.com/spxChrome
Carnophobia
Illustration by Rebecca Sutherland
Noctophobia
Moon, Viktar Malyshchyts/Shutterstock

Ailurophobia
Cat eyes, Voronin76/Shutterstock
Wiccaphobia
Witch's hat, jscmilly/Shutterstock
Climacophobia
Staircase, iStockphoto.com/nikada
Xyrophobia
Razor blade, R-studio/Shutterstock

Ornithophobia
Bird's nest, iStockphoto.com/malerapaso
Gnomophobia
Gnome, iStockphoto.com/stockbart
Pteridophobia
Ferns, susi/Shutterstock
All photography by John Ross studio.
With thanks to Tony and Shin.